EZ PLAY

GUITAR

EASY TO READ NOTES WITH TABLATURE

BEST OF

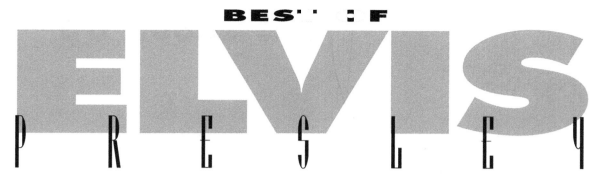

ELVIS PRESLEY

T0045105

Elvis and Elvis Presley are registered trademarks of Elvis Presley Enterprises, Inc., Copyright © 1992.

Photo Courtesy of Elvis Presley Enterprises, Inc.

ISBN 978-0-7395-1678-0

HAL•LEONARD®
CORPORATION
7777 W. BLUEMOUND RD. P.O. BOX 13819 MILWAUKEE, WI 53213

All Shook Up

Strum Pattern: 2
Pick Pattern: 4

Words and Music by Otis Blackwell
and Elvis Presley

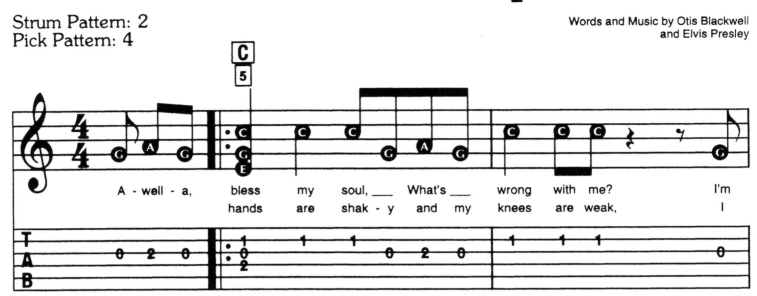

A - well - a, bless my soul, ___ What's ___ wrong with me? I'm
hands are shak - y and my knees are weak,   I

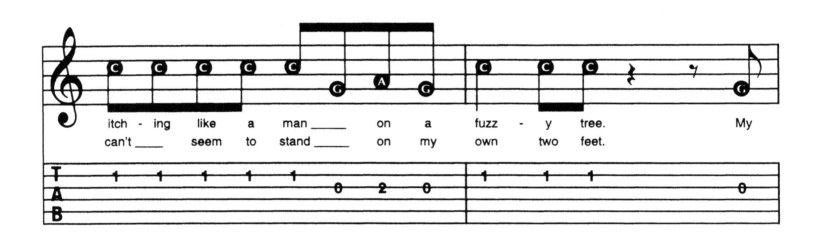

itch - ing like a man ___ on a fuzz - y tree.   My
can't ___ seem to stand ___ on my own two feet.

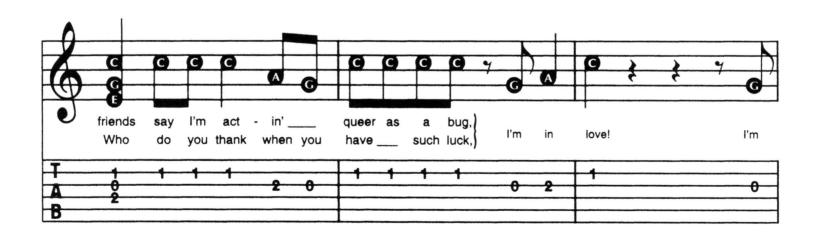

friends say I'm act - in' ___ queer as a bug,⎞ I'm in love!   I'm
Who do you thank when you have ___ such luck,⎠

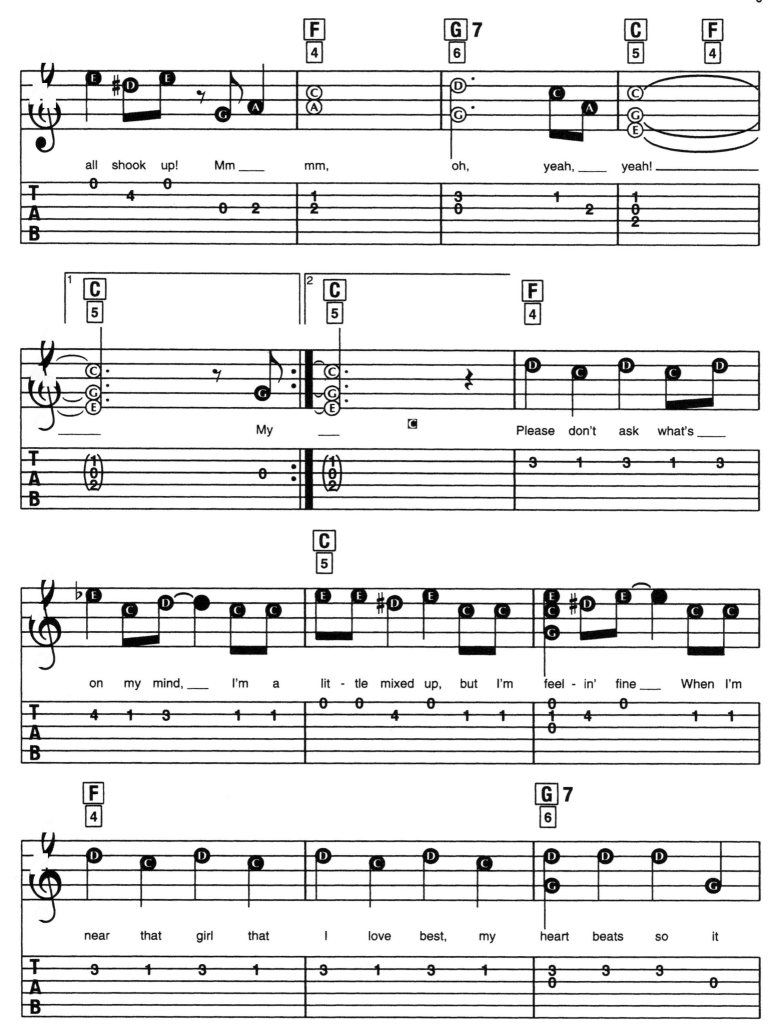

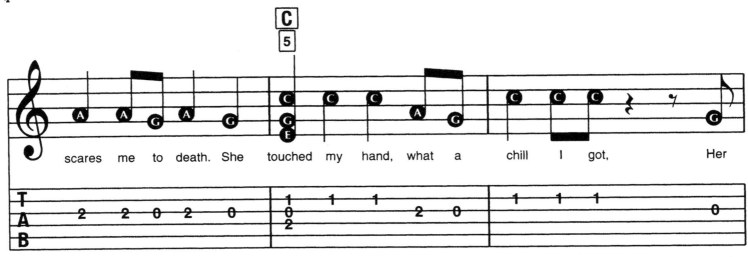

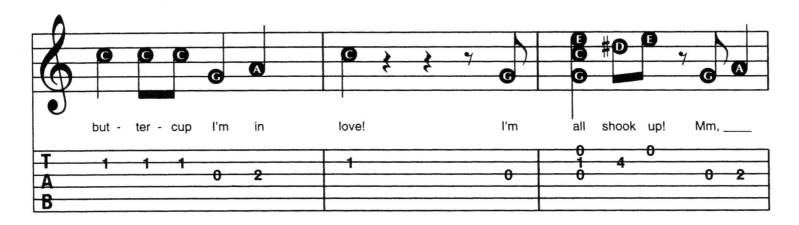

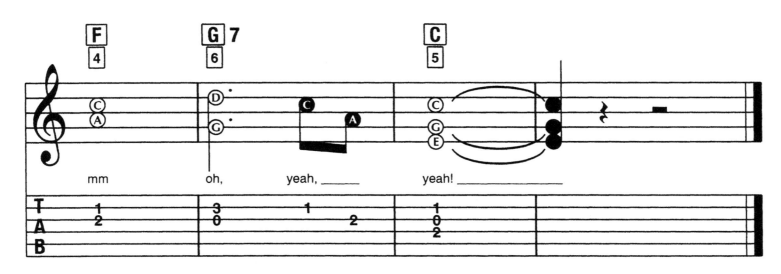

Are You Lonesome Tonight?

Strum Pattern: 8
Pick Pattern: 8

Words and Music by Roy Turk
and Lou Handman

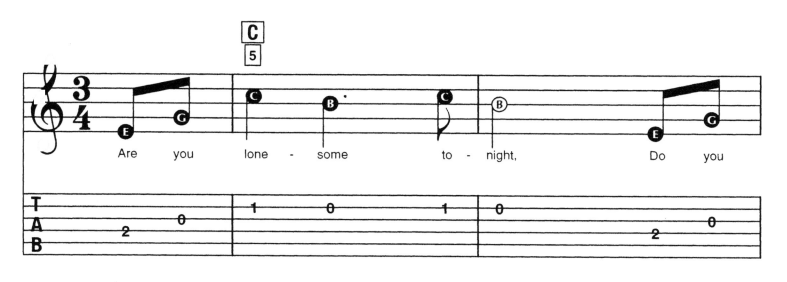

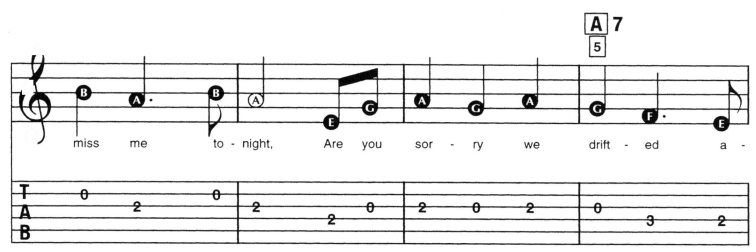

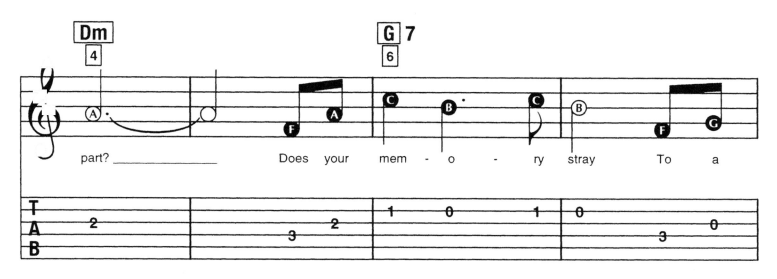

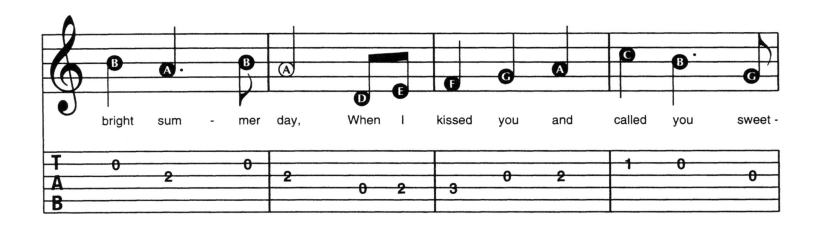

bright sum - mer day, When I kissed you and called you sweet -

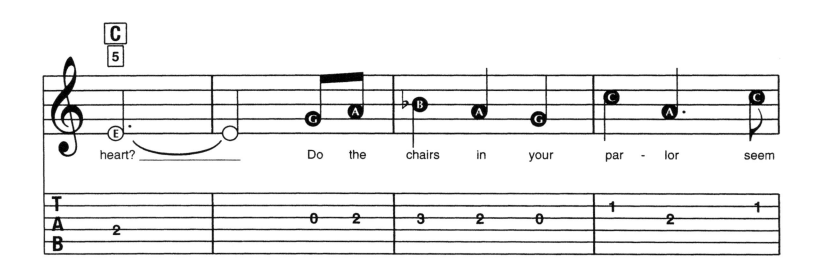

heart? _____ Do the chairs in your par - lor seem

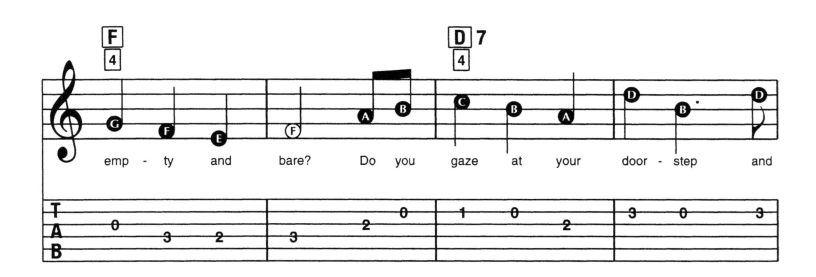

emp - ty and bare? Do you gaze at your door - step and

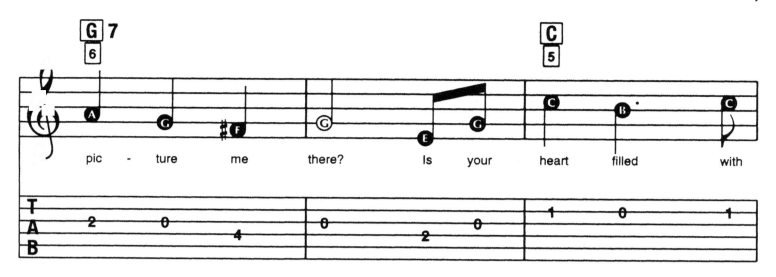

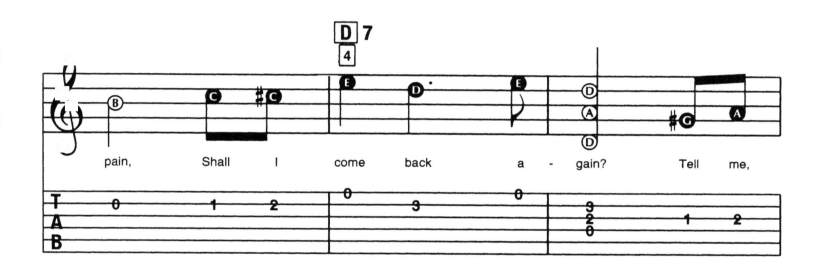

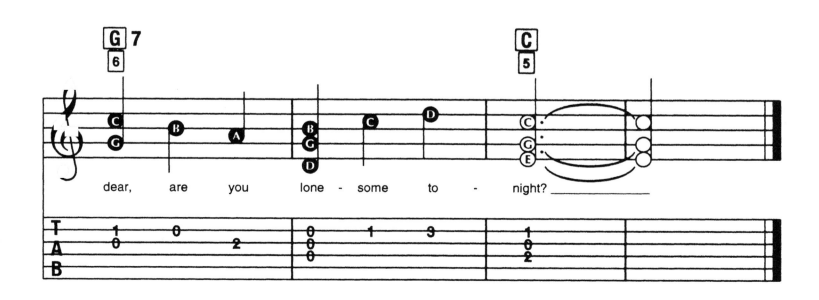

Blue Suede Shoes

Strum Pattern: 5
Pick Pattern: 4

Words and Music by
Carl Lee Perkins

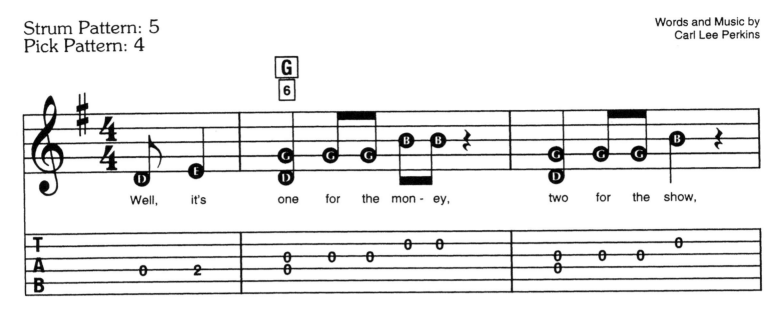

Well, it's one for the mon - ey, two for the show,

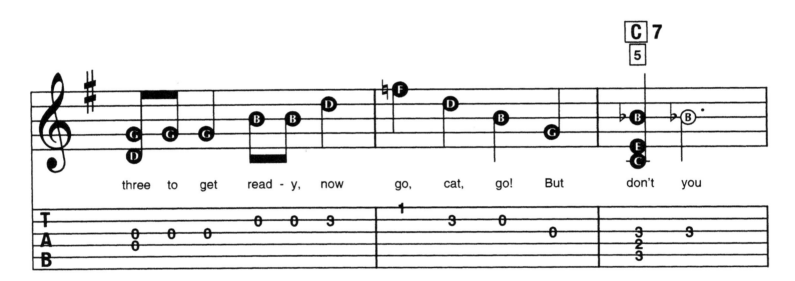

three to get read - y, now go, cat, go! But don't you

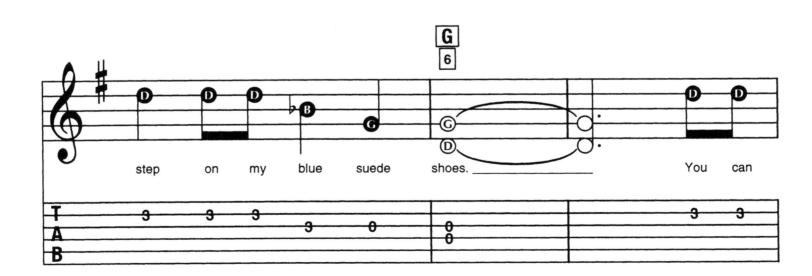

step on my blue suede shoes. _____ You can

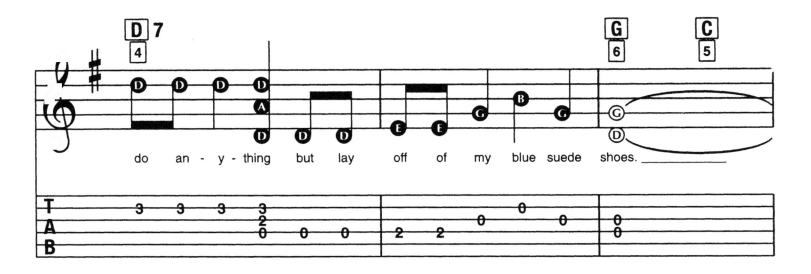

do an - y - thing but lay off of my blue suede shoes. _____

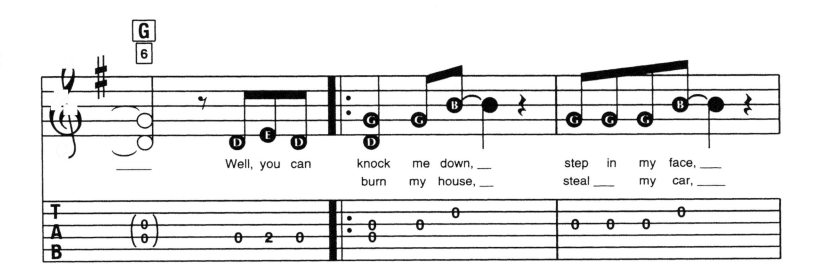

____ Well, you can knock me down, __ step in my face, __
burn my house, __ steal ___ my car, ____

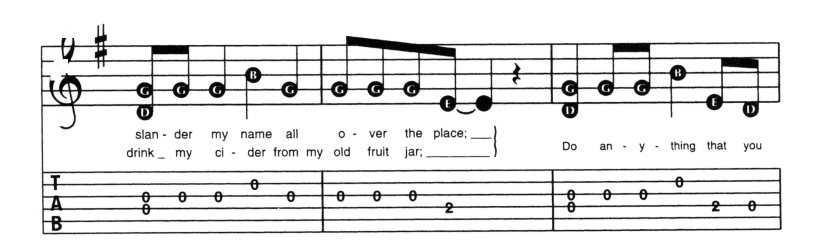

slan - der my name all o - ver the place; ___
drink _ my ci - der from my old fruit jar; _____

Do an - y - thing that you

Can't Help Falling In Love

Strum Pattern: 2
Pick Pattern: 4

Words and Music by George David Weiss,
Hugo Peretti, and Luigi Creatore

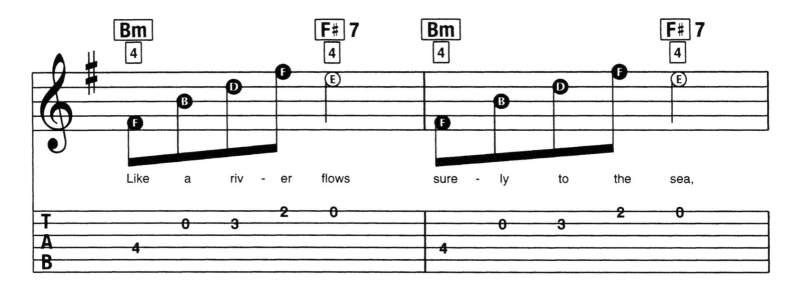

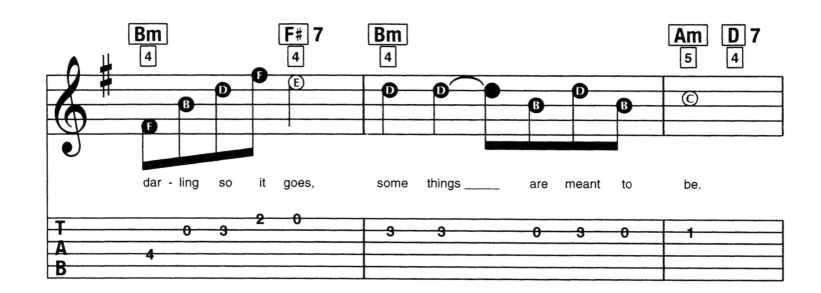

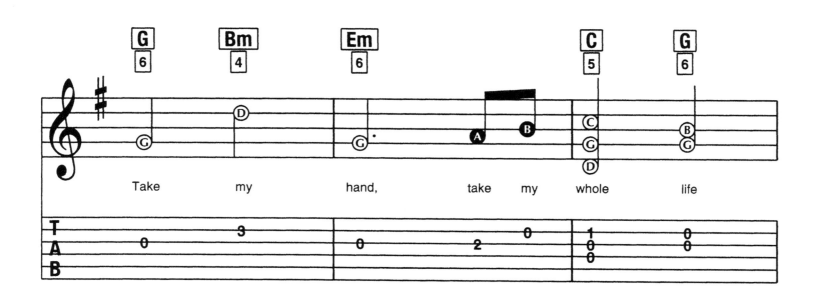

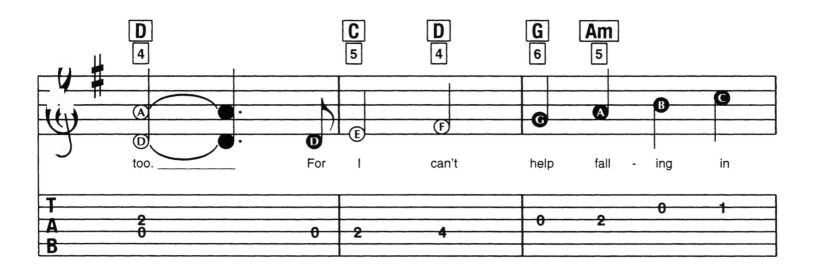

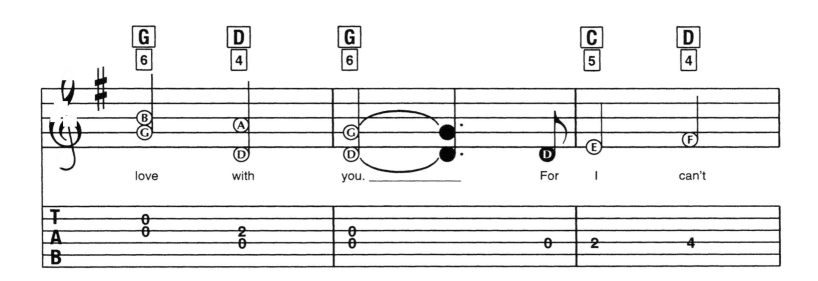

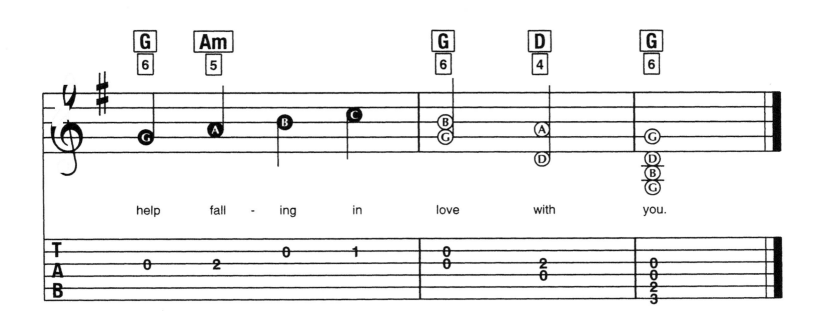

Crying In The Chapel

Strum Pattern: 1
Pick Pattern: 2

Words and Music by
Artie Glenn

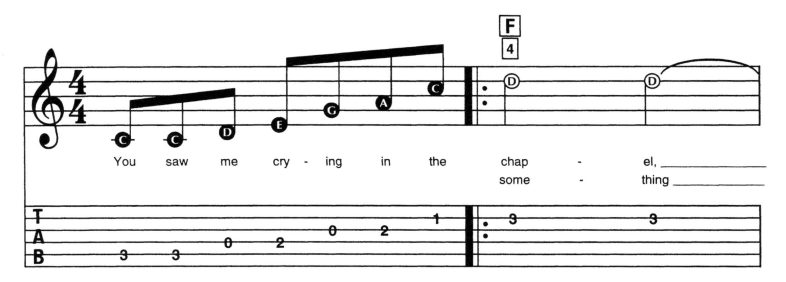

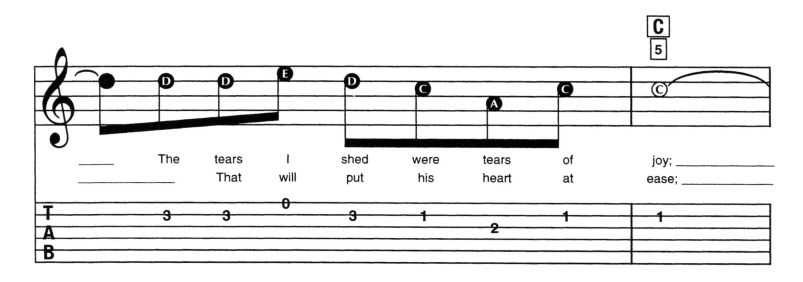

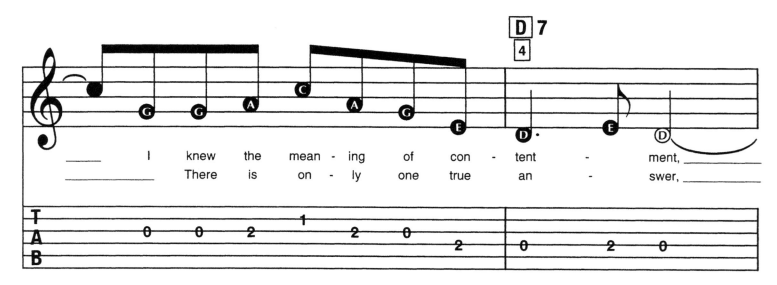

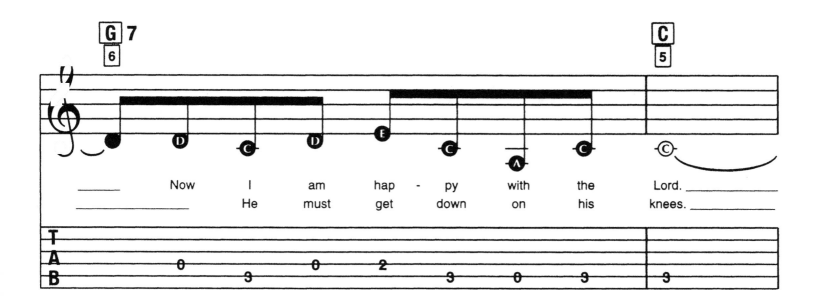

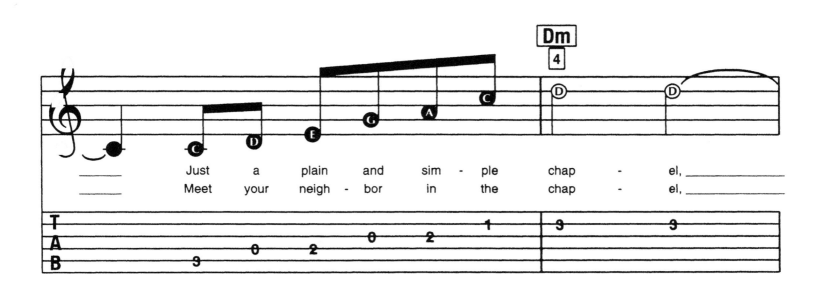

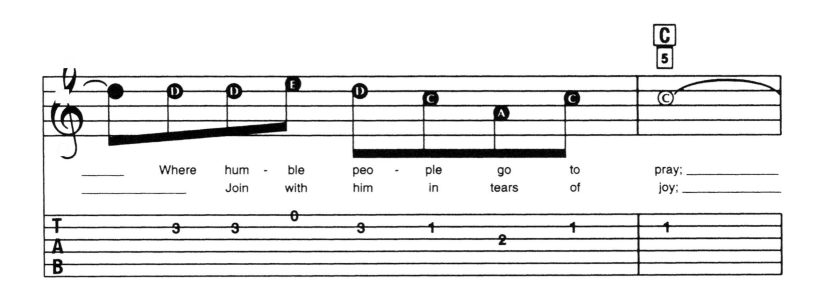

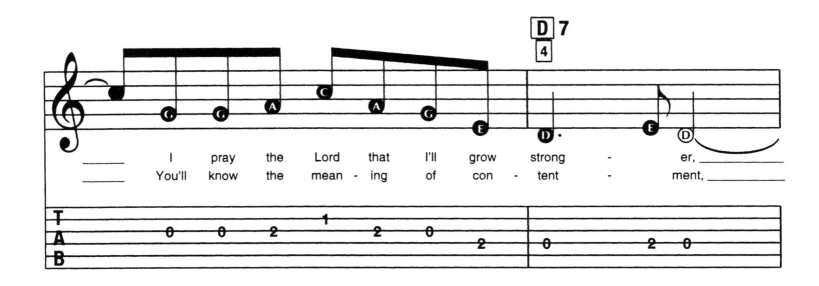

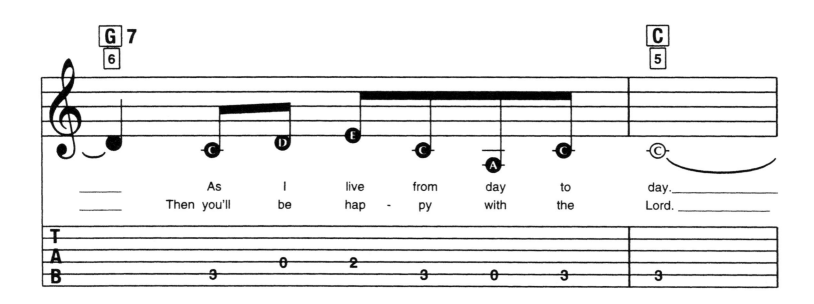

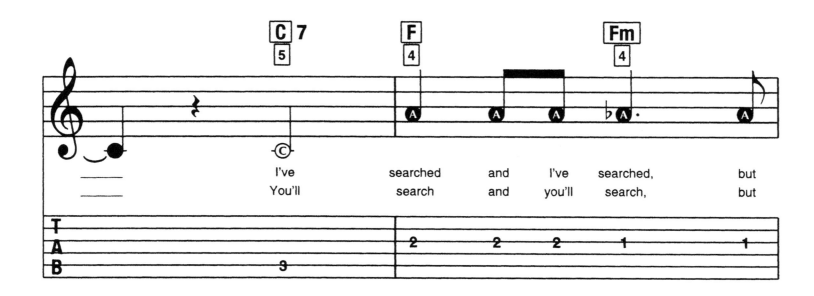

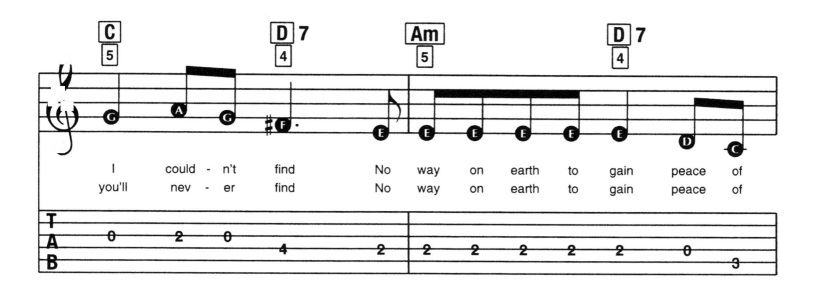

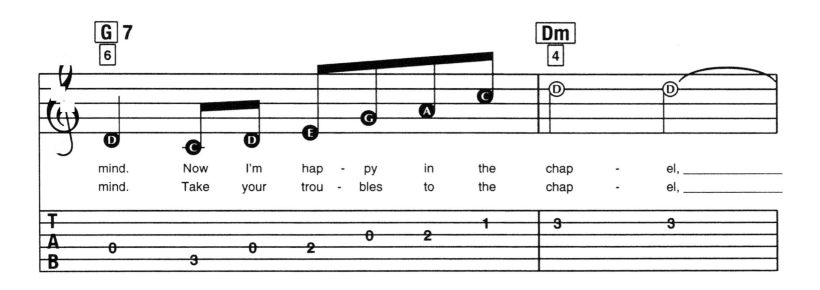

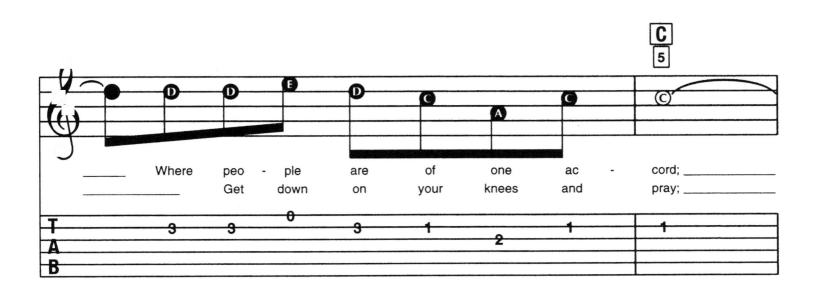

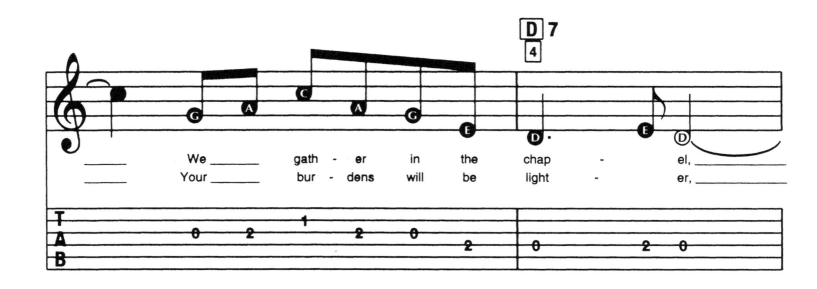

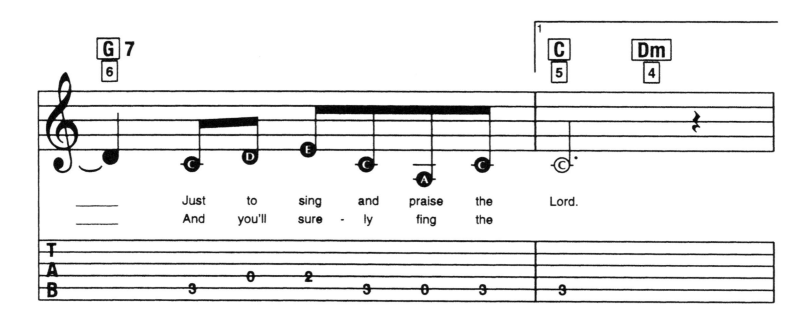

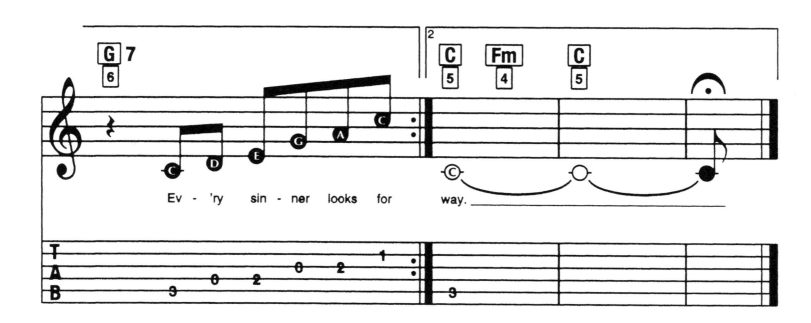

Don't Be Cruel
(To A Heart That's True)

Strum Pattern: 2
Pick Pattern: 4

Words and Music by Otis Blackwell
and Elvis Presley

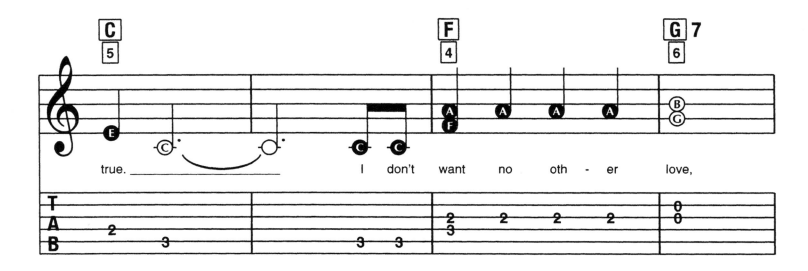

true. _____ I don't want no oth - er love,

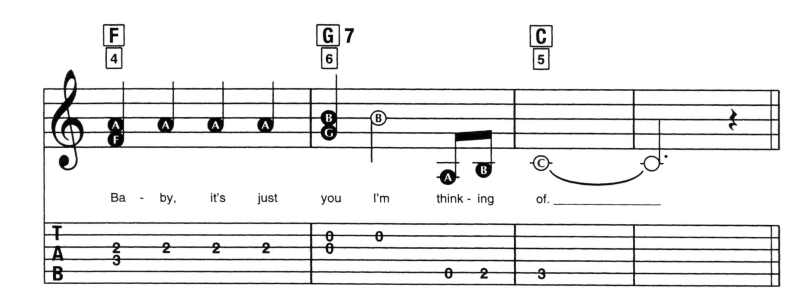

Ba - by, it's just you I'm think - ing of. _____

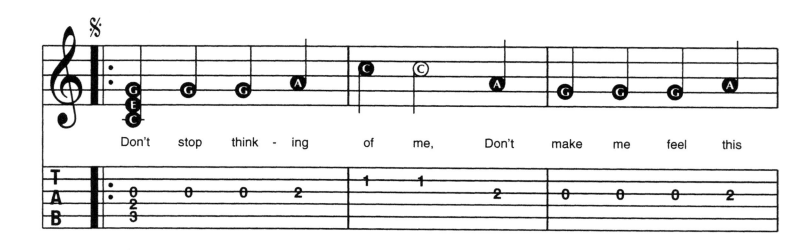

Don't stop think - ing of me, Don't make me feel this

G.I. Blues

Strum Pattern: 1
Pick Pattern: 2

Words and Music by Sid Tepper
and Roy C. Bennett

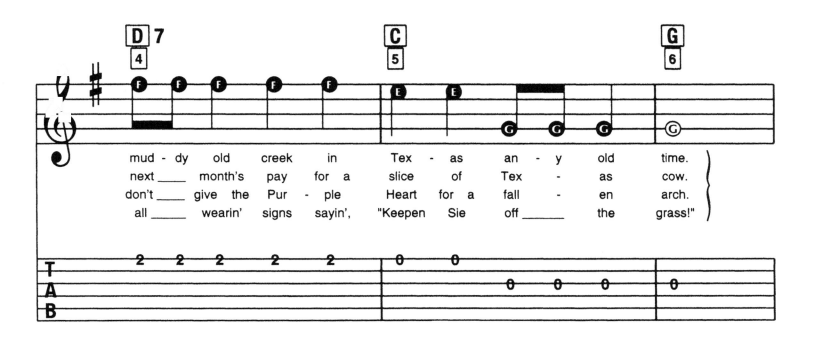

mud - dy   old   creek   in   Tex - as   an - y   old   time.
next ____ month's   pay   for a   slice   of   Tex -   as   cow.
don't ____ give the Pur - ple   Heart   for a   fall -   en   arch.
all ____ wearin'   signs   sayin', "Keepen Sie   off ____   the   grass!"

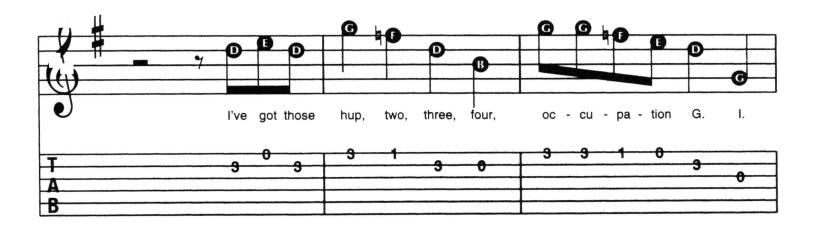

I've got those   hup, two,   three, four,   oc - cu - pa - tion G.   I.

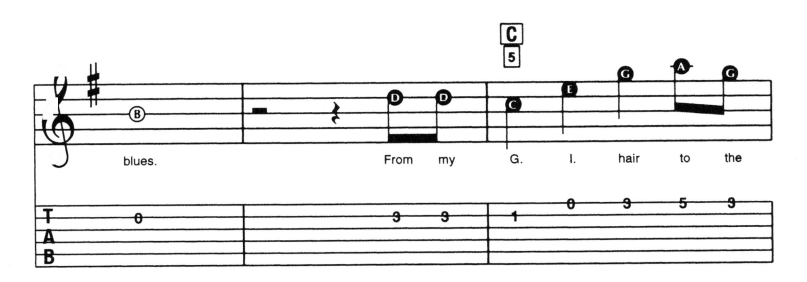

blues.   From   my   G.   I.   hair   to   the

24

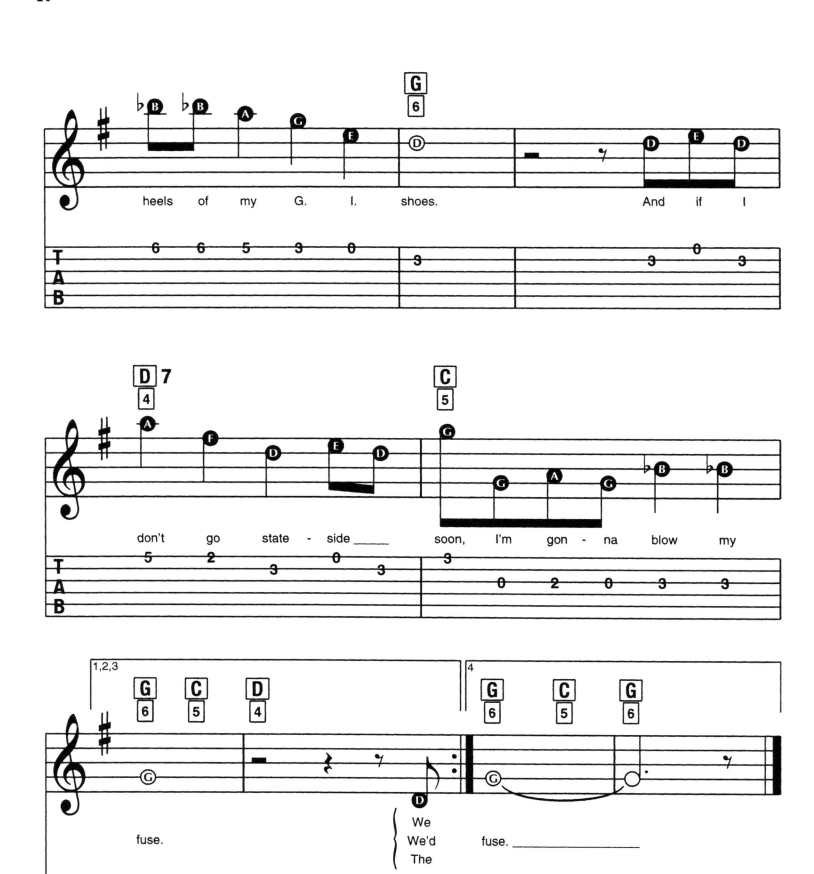

Heartbreak Hotel

Strum Pattern: 5
Pick Pattern: 4

By Mae Boren Axton,
Tommy Durden and Elvis Presley

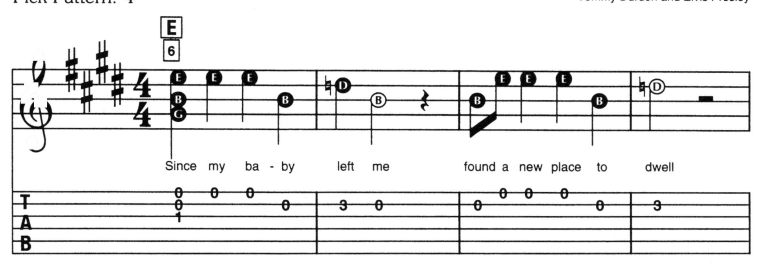

Since my ba - by left me   found a new place to   dwell

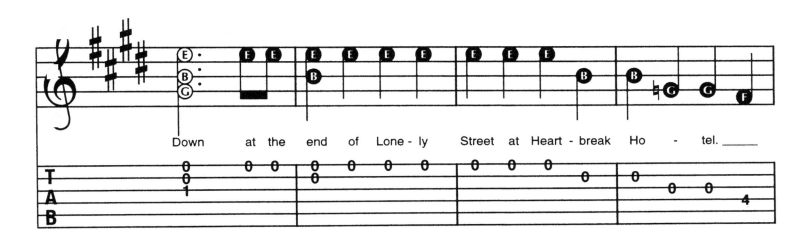

Down   at the end of Lone - ly   Street at Heart - break Ho - tel. _____

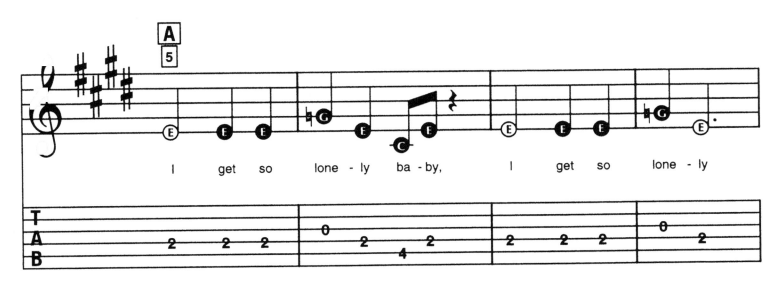

I   get so   lone - ly   ba - by,   I   get so   lone - ly

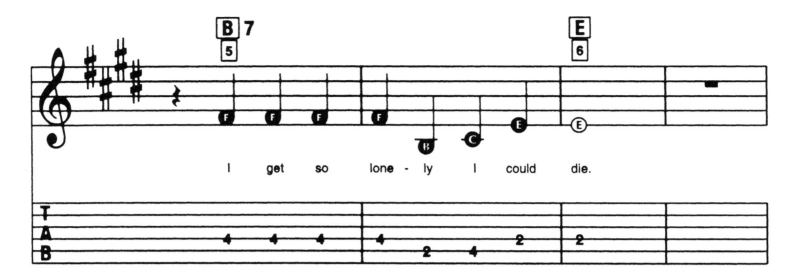

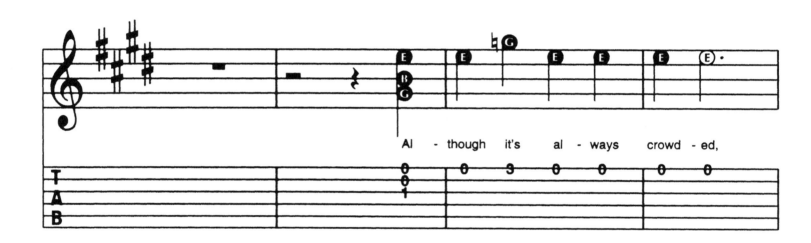

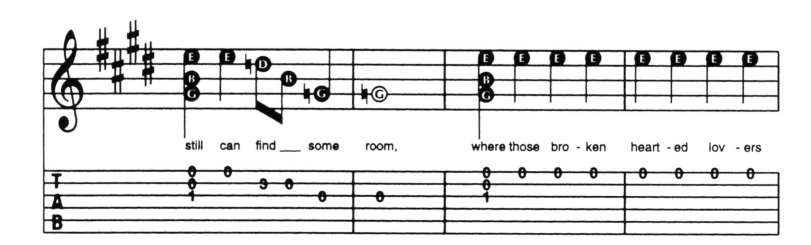

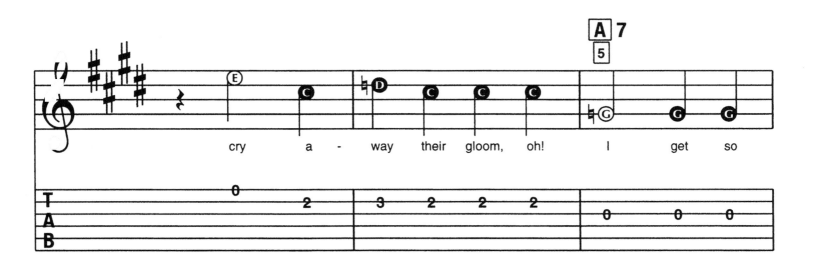

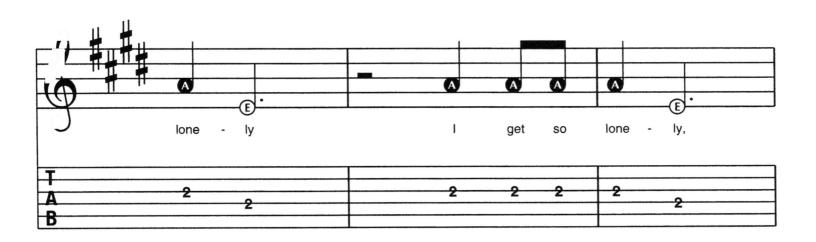

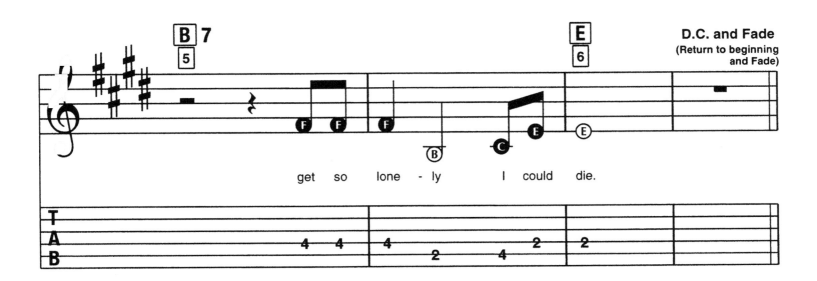

Hound Dog

Strum Pattern: 1
Pick Pattern: 2

Words and Music by Jerry Leiber
and Mike Stoller

MCA music publishing

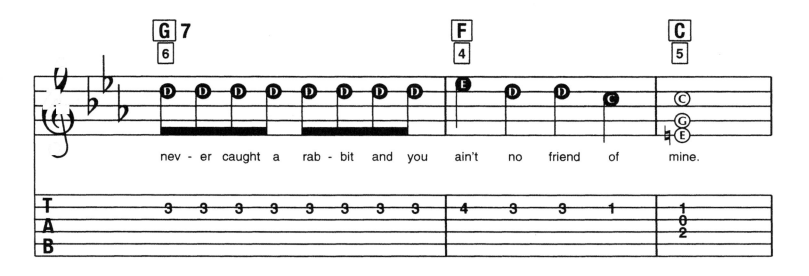

nev - er caught a rab - bit and you ain't no friend of mine.

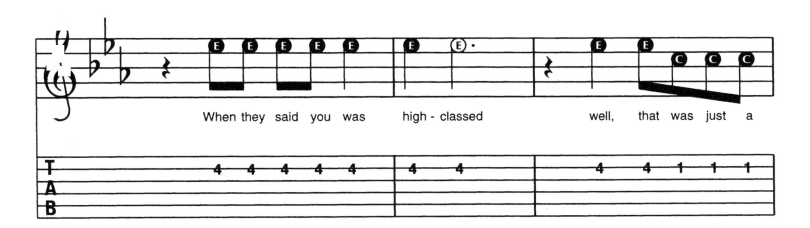

When they said you was high - classed well, that was just a

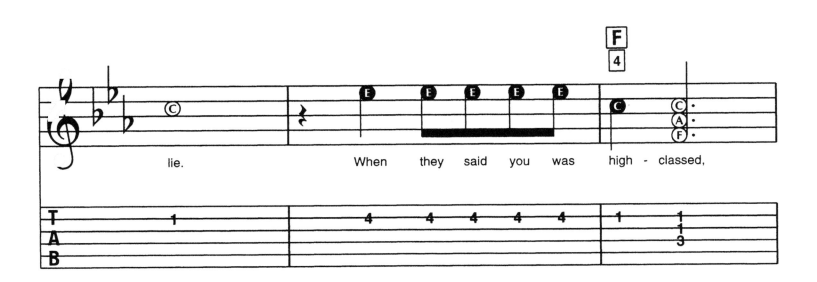

lie. When they said you was high - classed,

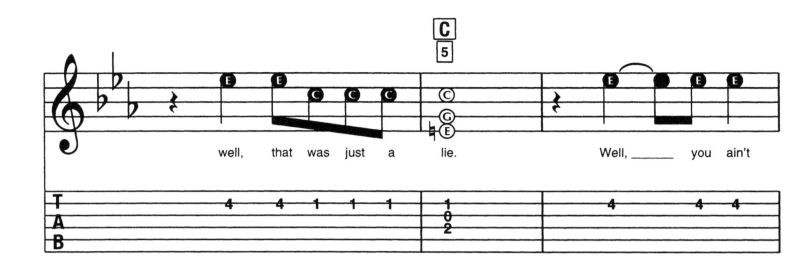

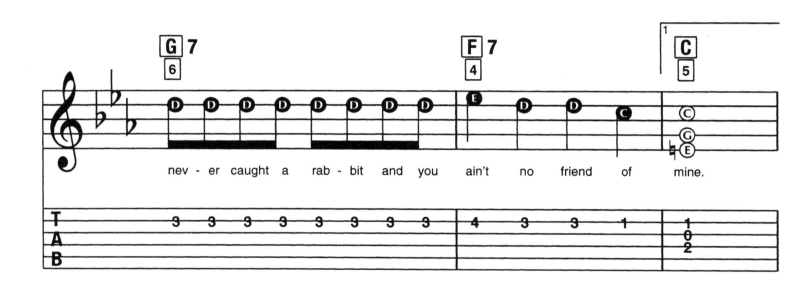

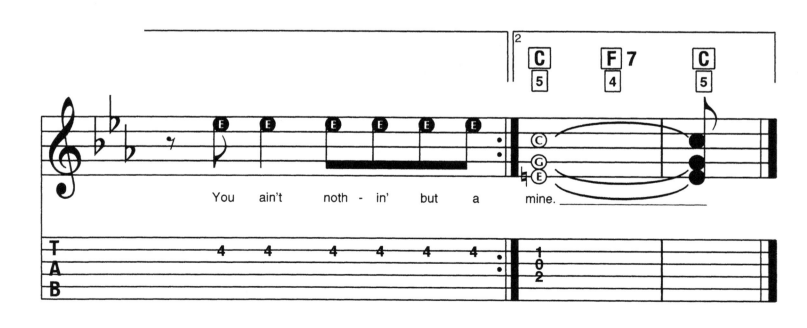

King Creole

Strum Pattern: 1
Pick Pattern: 2

Words and Music by Jerry Leiber
and Mike Stoller

There's a man in New Or - leans who plays _____
plays _____ some - thing e - vil then he

rock and roll. He's a gui - tar man _____ with a
plays something sweet. No _____ mat - ter what he plays you got to

great big soul. _____ He lays down a beat _____ like a
get up on your feet. When he gets the rock - in' fev - er, ba - by

32

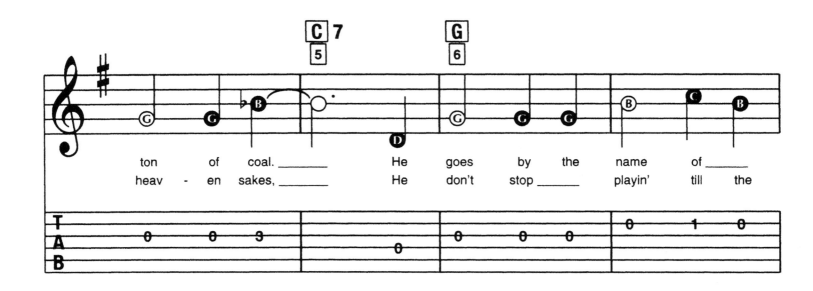

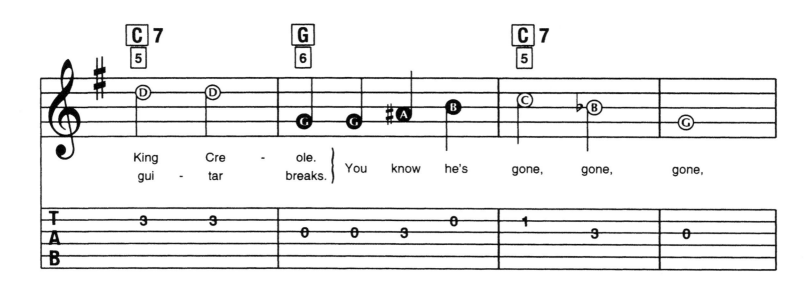

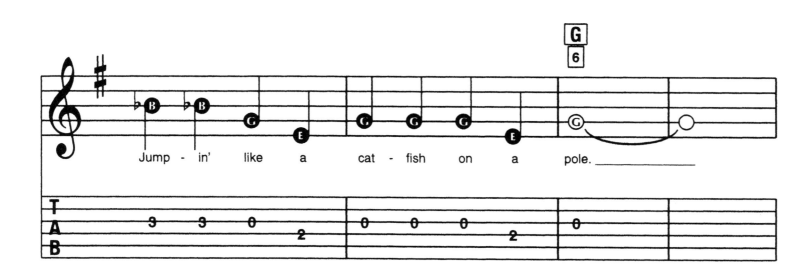

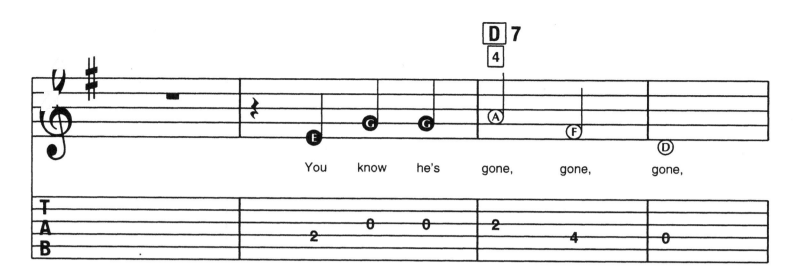

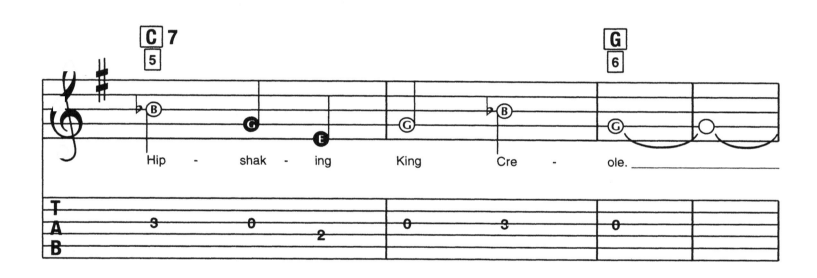

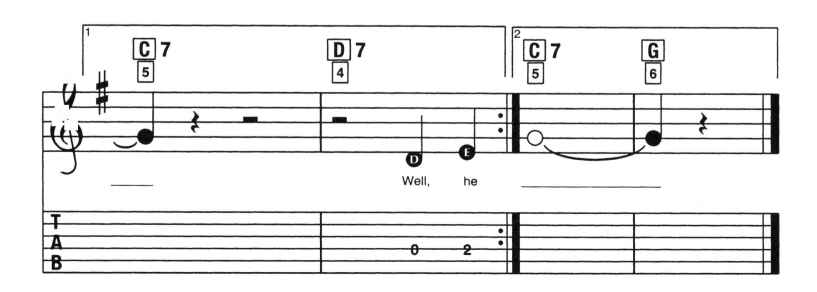

It's Now Or Never

Strum Pattern: 1
Pick Pattern: 2

Words and Music by Aaron Schroeder
and Wally Gold

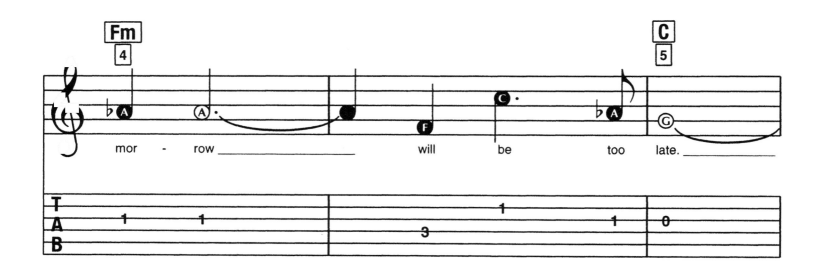

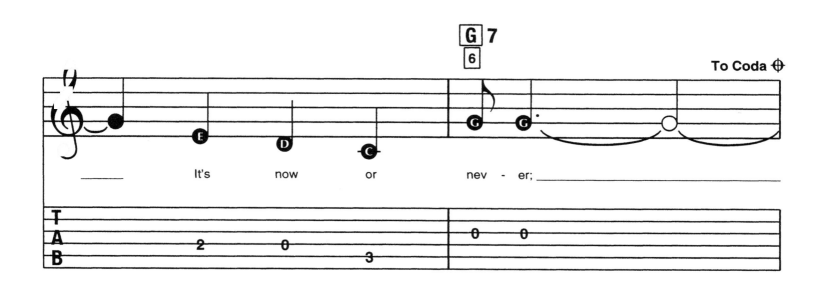

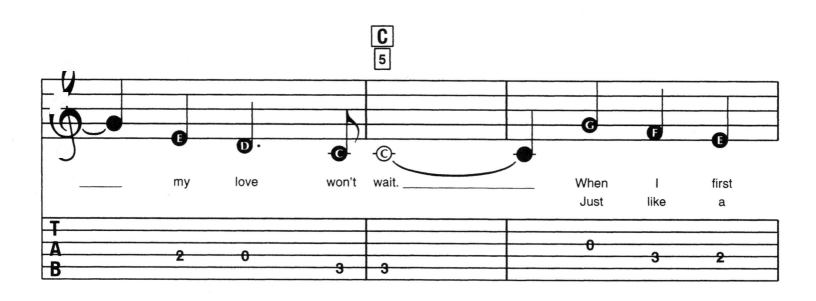

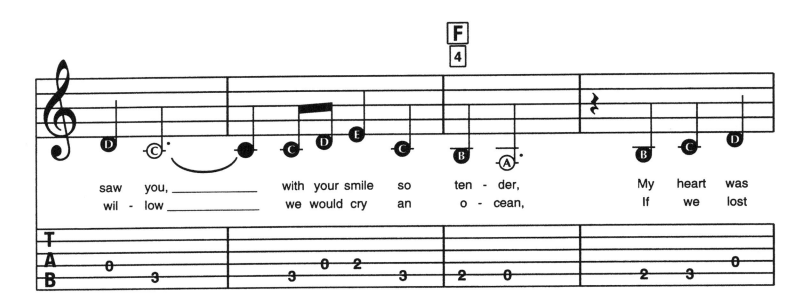

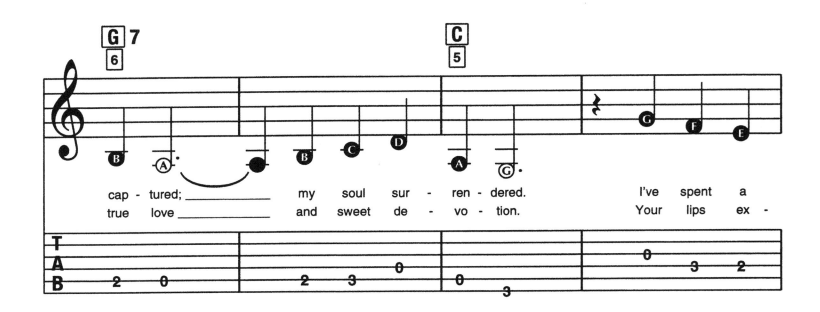

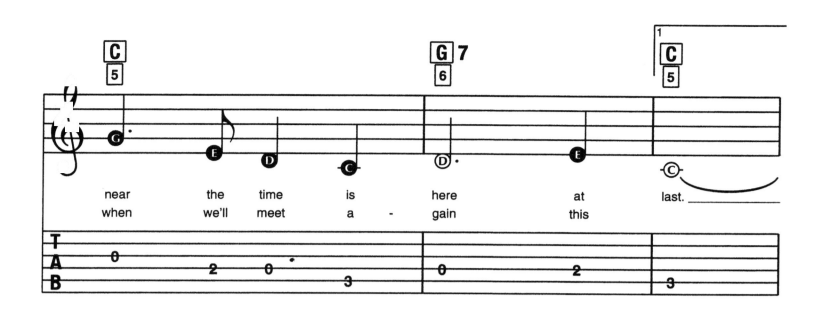

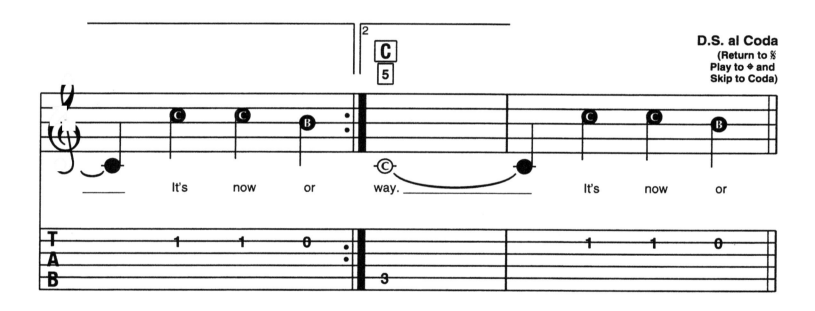

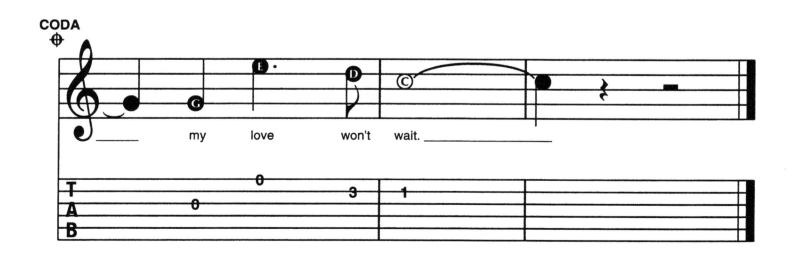

Jailhouse Rock

Strum Pattern: 1
Pick Pattern: 2

Words and Music by Jerry Leiber
and Mike Stoller

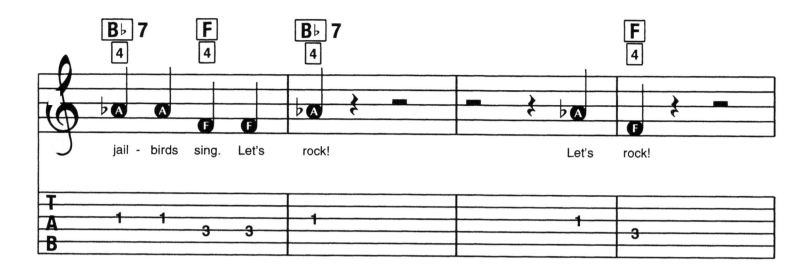

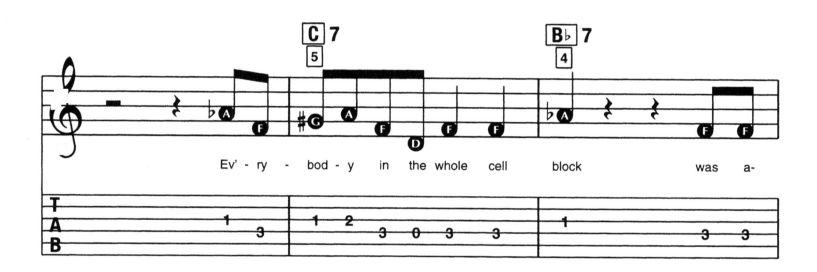

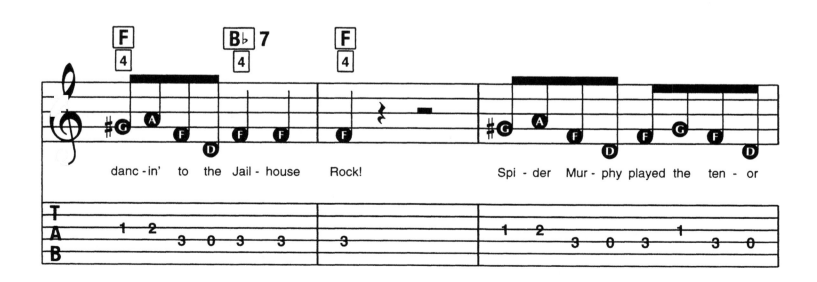

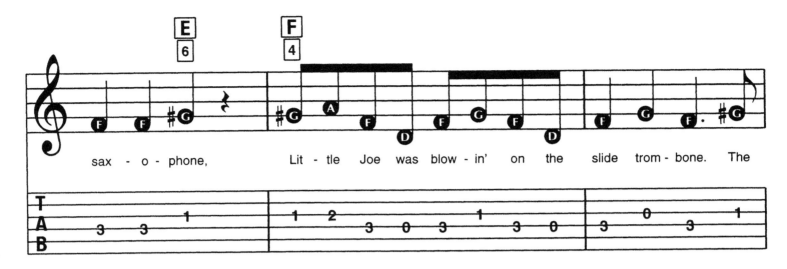

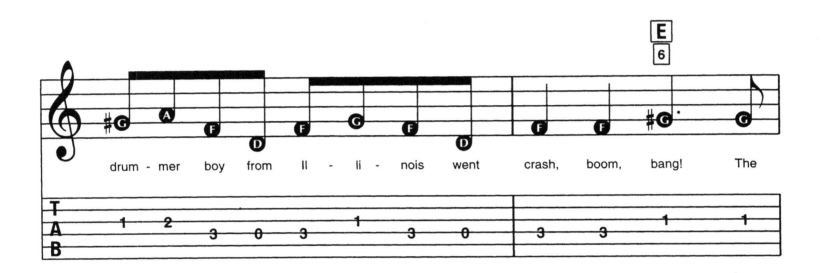

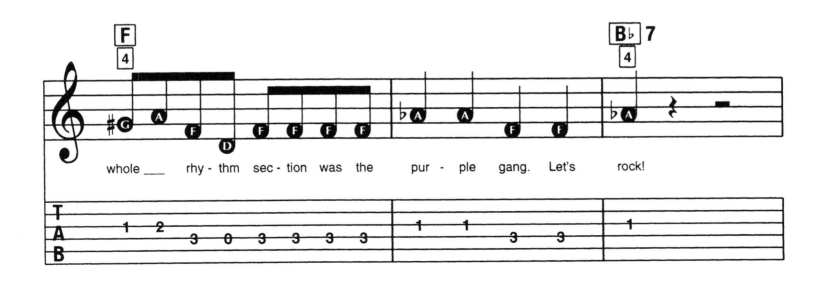

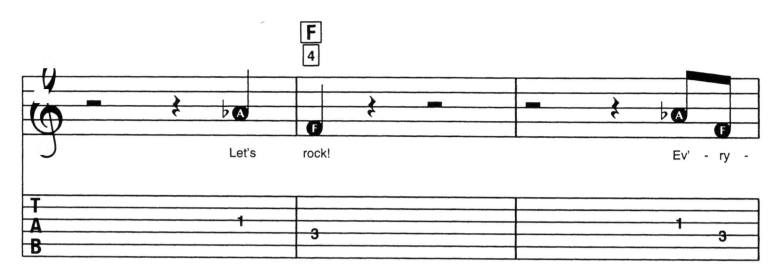

Let's rock! Ev' - ry -

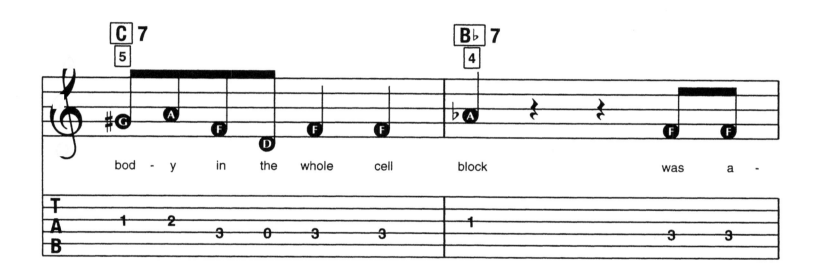

bod - y in the whole cell block was a -

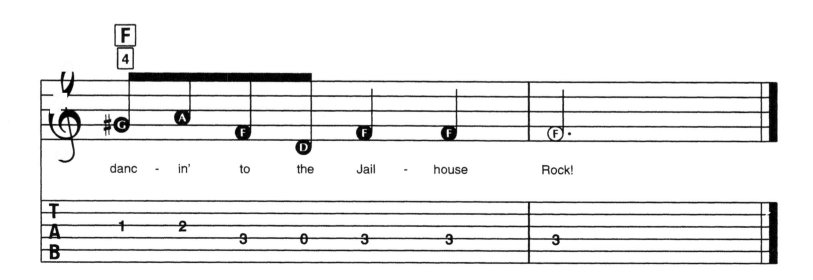

danc - in' to the Jail - house Rock!

Little Sister

Strum Pattern: 1
Pick Pattern: 3

Words and Music by Doc Pomus
and Mort Shuman

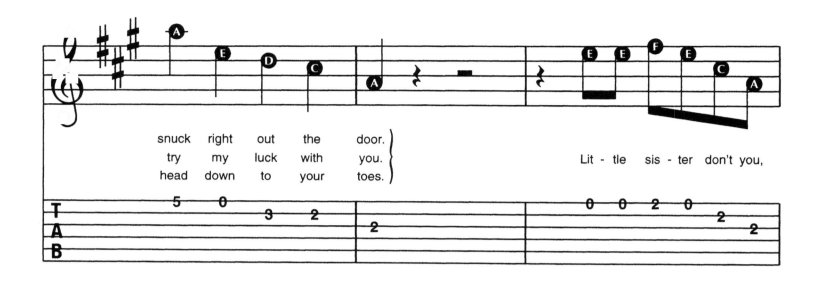

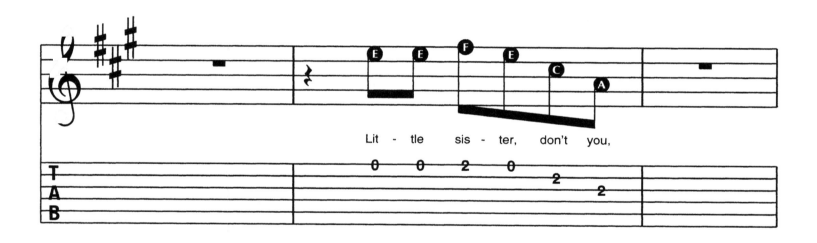

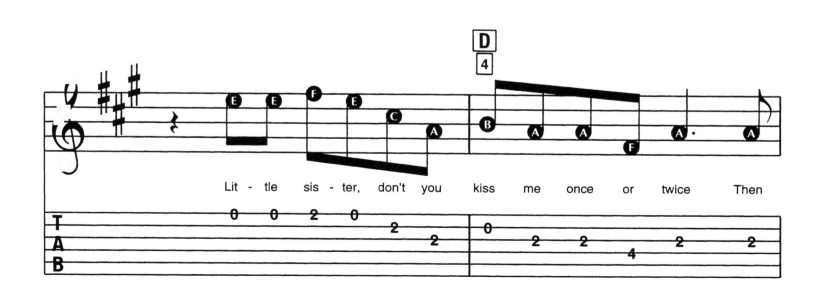

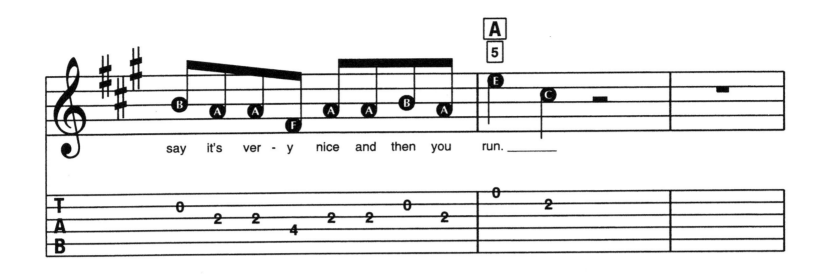

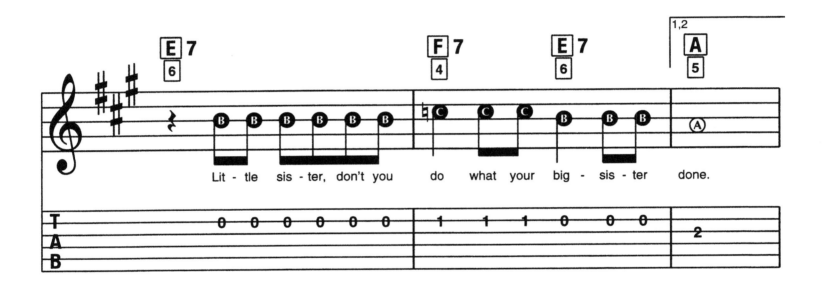

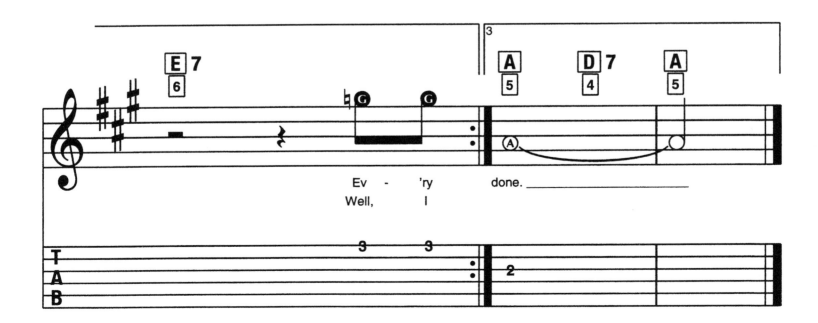

Love Me Tender

Strum Pattern: 4
Pick Pattern: 9

Words and Music by Elvis Presley
and Vera Matson

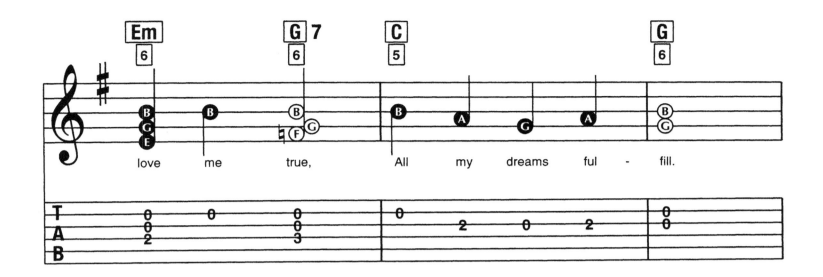

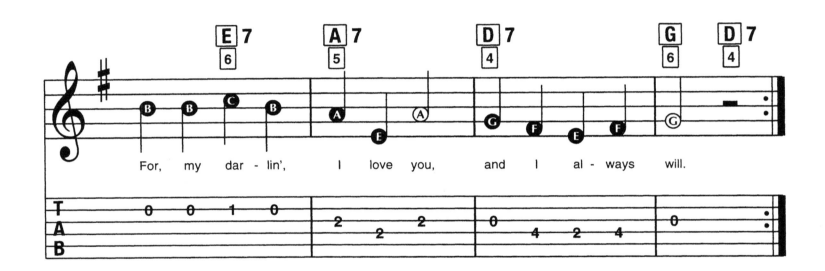

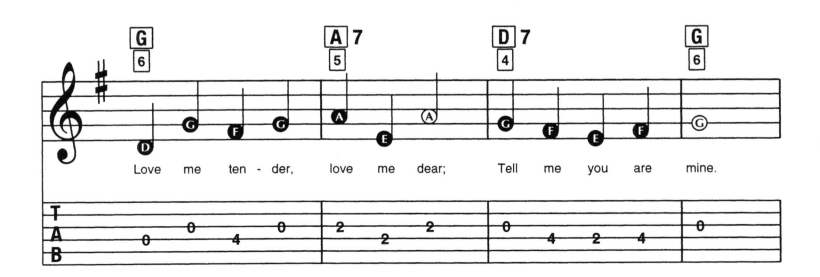

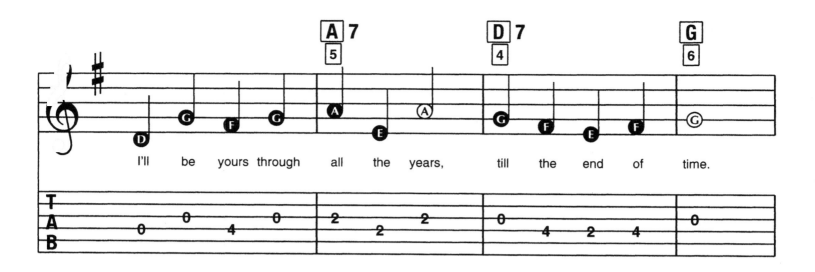

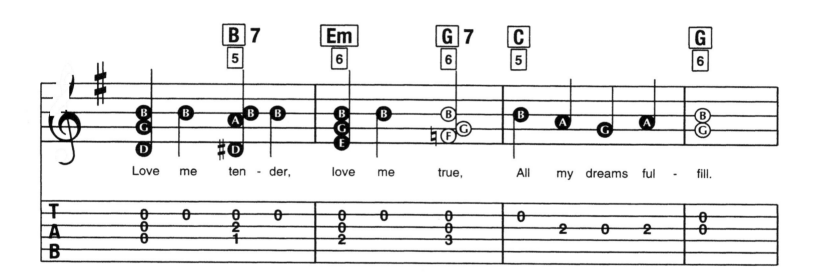

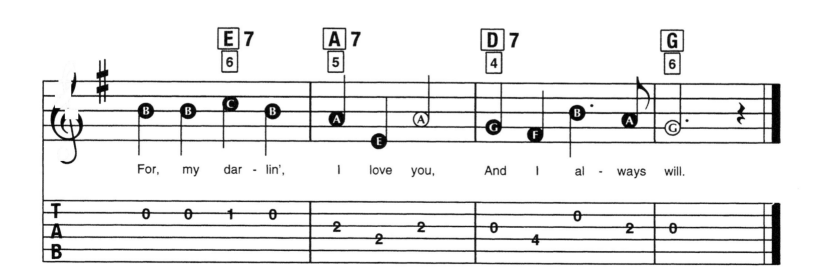

Return To Sender

Strum Pattern: 1
Pick Pattern: 2

Words and Music by Otis Blackwell
and Winfield Scott

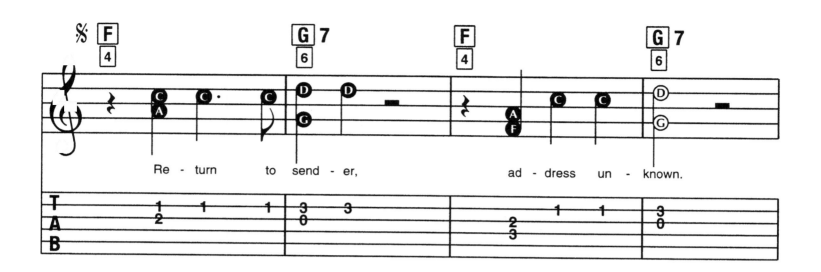

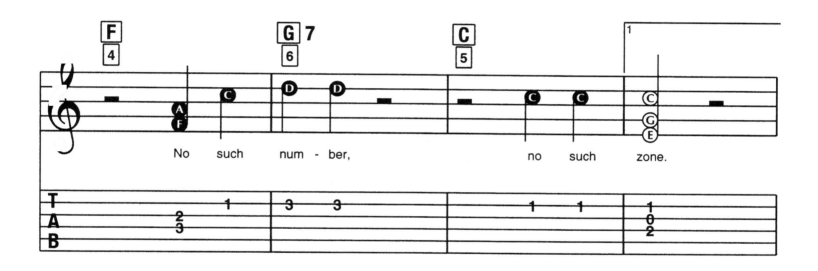

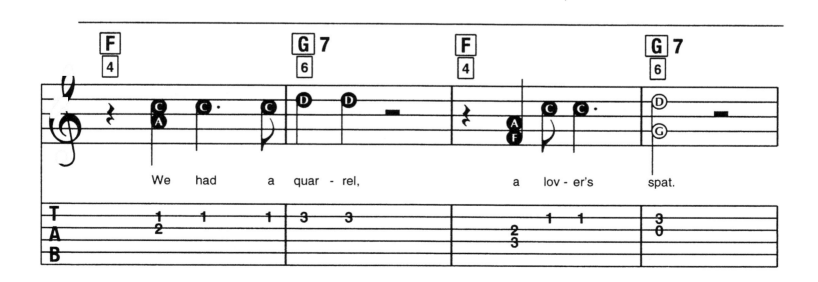

(Let Me Be Your)
Teddy Bear

Strum Pattern: 1
Pick Pattern: 2

Words and Music by Kal Mann
and Bernie Lowe

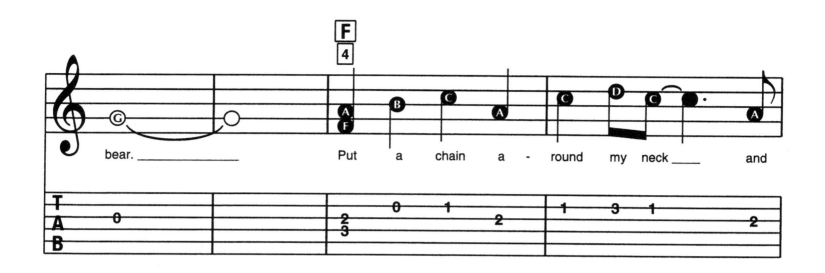

bear. _____ Put a chain a - round my neck _____ and

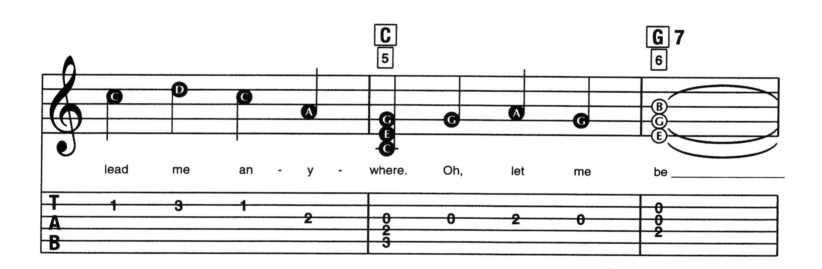

lead me an - y - where. Oh, let me be _____

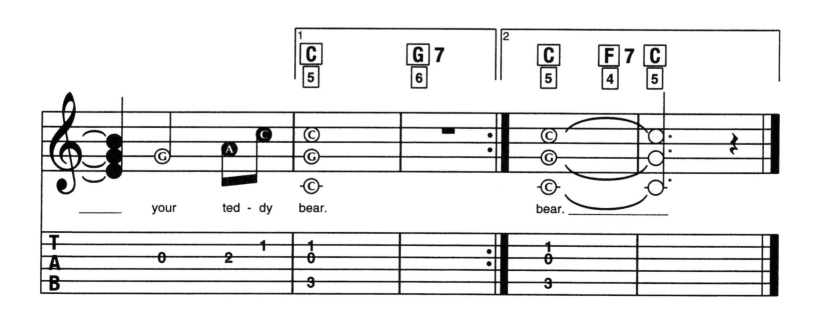

_____ your ted - dy bear. bear. _____

Wear My Ring Around Your Neck

Strum Pattern: 2
Pick Pattern: 4

Words and Music by Bert Carroll
and Russell Moody

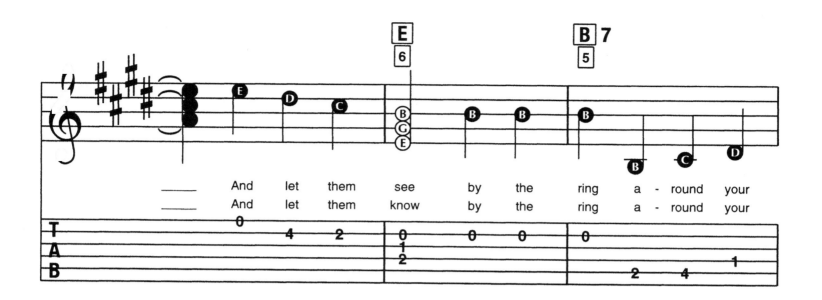

And let them see by the ring a - round your
And let them know by the ring a - round your

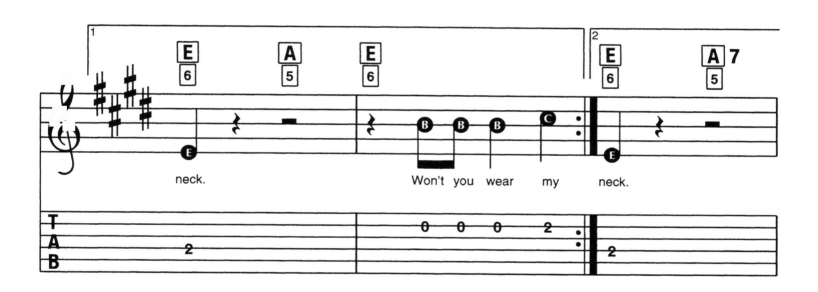

neck. Won't you wear my neck.

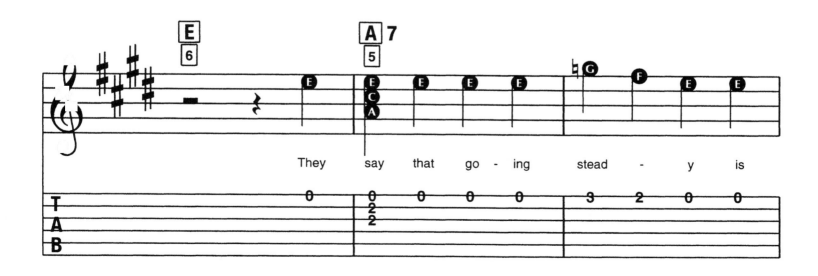

They say that go - ing stead - y is

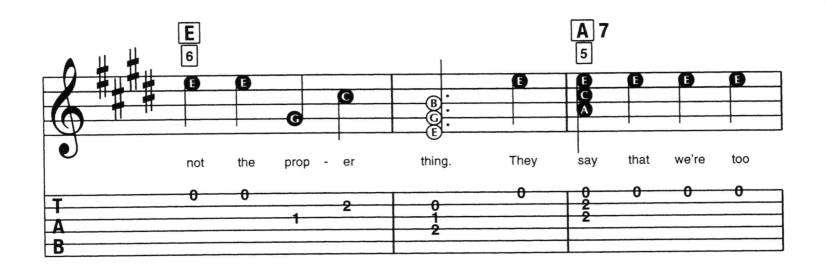

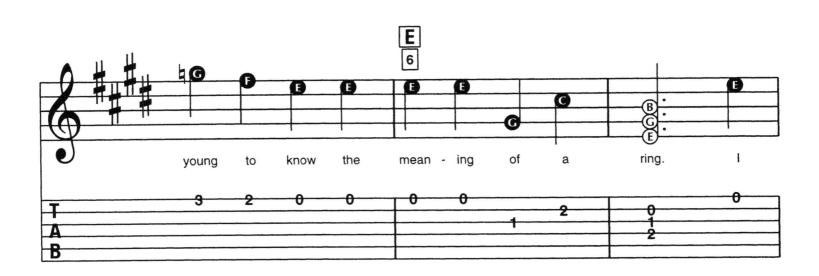

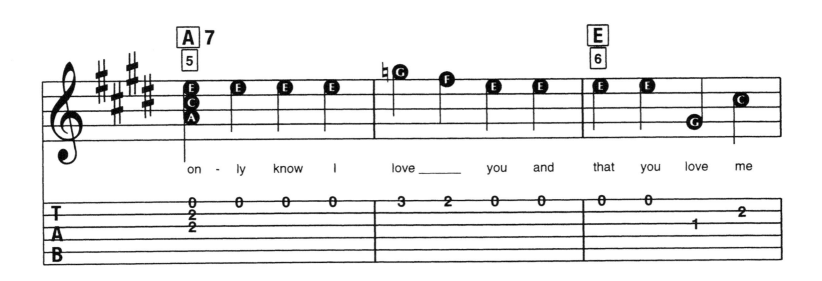

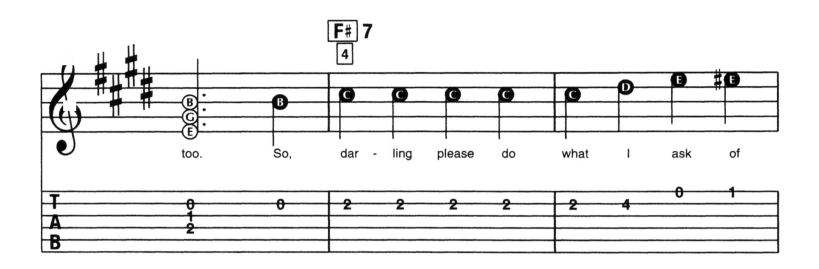

too. So, dar - ling please do what I ask of

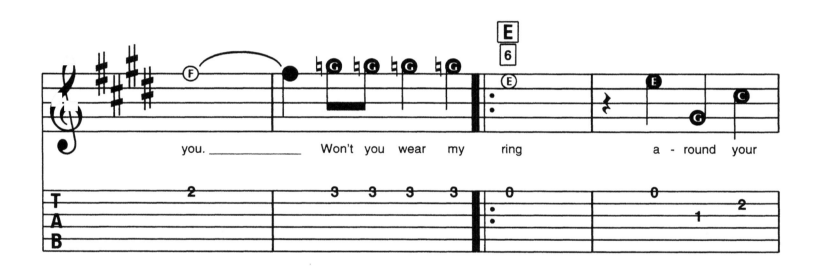

you. _____ Won't you wear my ring a - round your

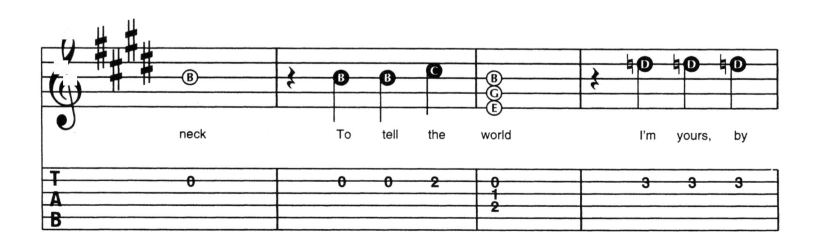

neck To tell the world I'm yours, by

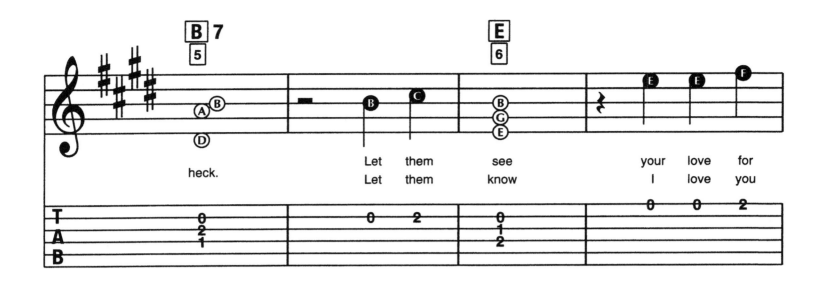

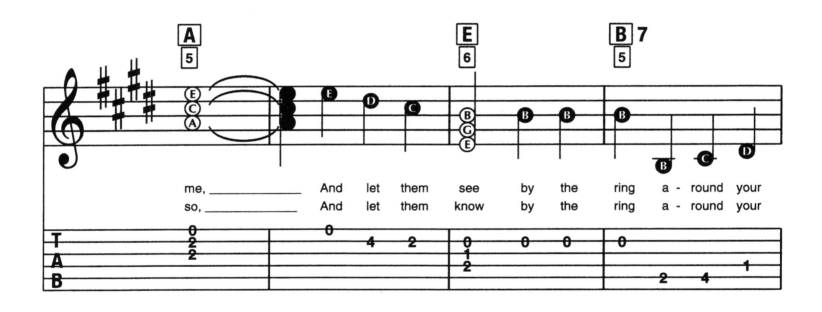

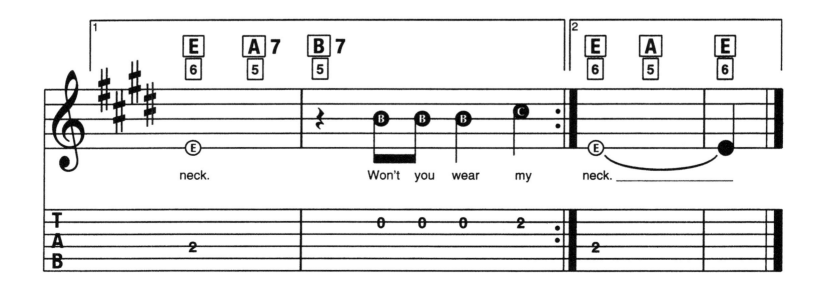

Wooden Heart

Strum Pattern: 3
Pick Pattern: 3

Words and Music by Fred Wise, Ben Weisman,
Kay Twomey and Berthold Kaempfert

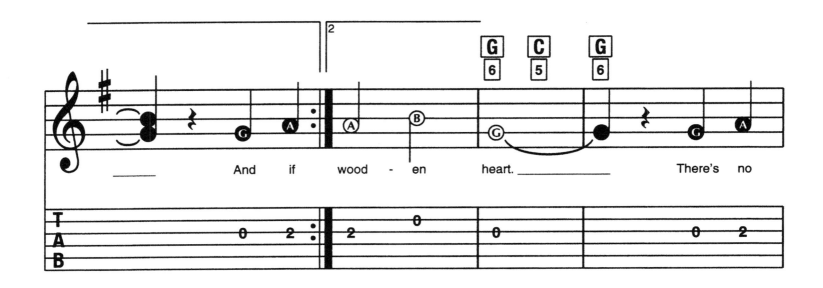

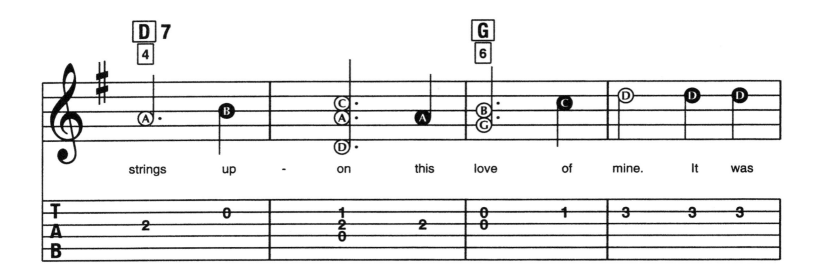

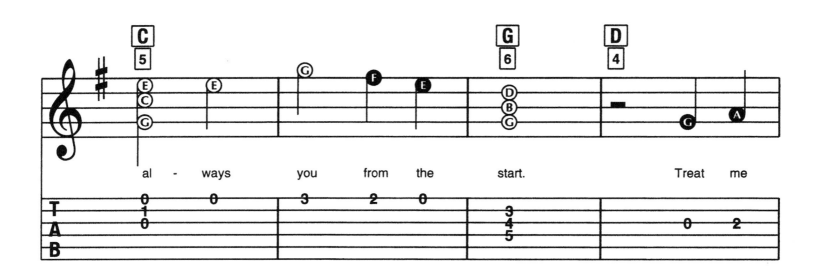

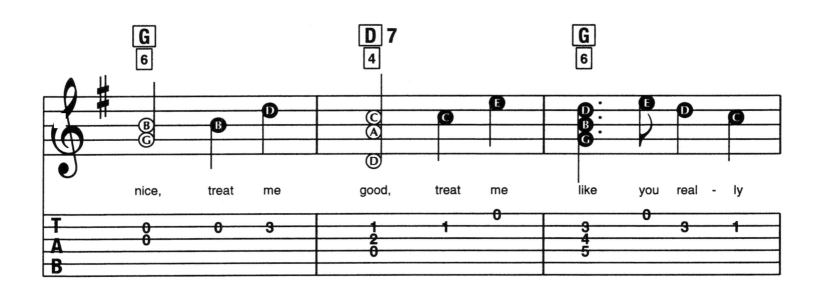

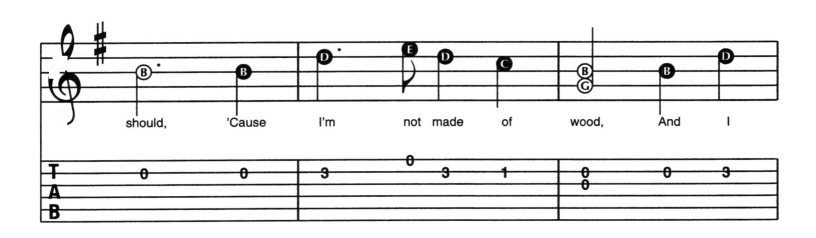

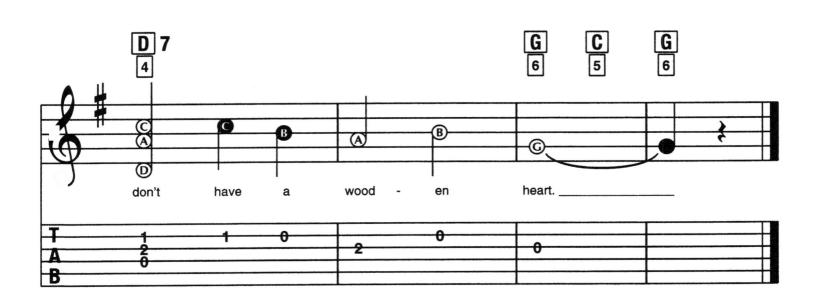

USING THE PICKING AND STRUM PATTERNS

Below each of the chord symbols in the music are numbers that correspond to the lowest string for each chord. For example, below the C chord symbol is a five. The lowest string that you should play when playing a C chord is the fifth string.

When using a Picking Pattern, pick the lowest string (shown by the number below the chord symbol) with your thumb. The letters in the Picking Pattern show which right hand finger plays which string. The fingers are labeled as follows:

p: thumb
i: index finger
m: middle finger
a: ring finger

For example, Picking Pattern 1 is to be played: thumb - middle/ring - thumb - index - middle/ring

Strum Pattern

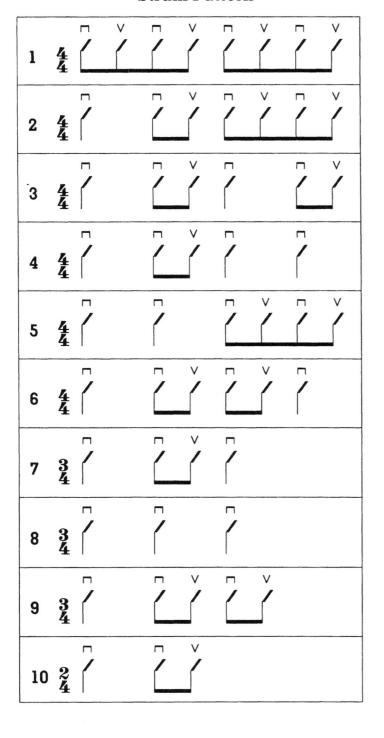

Picking Pattern

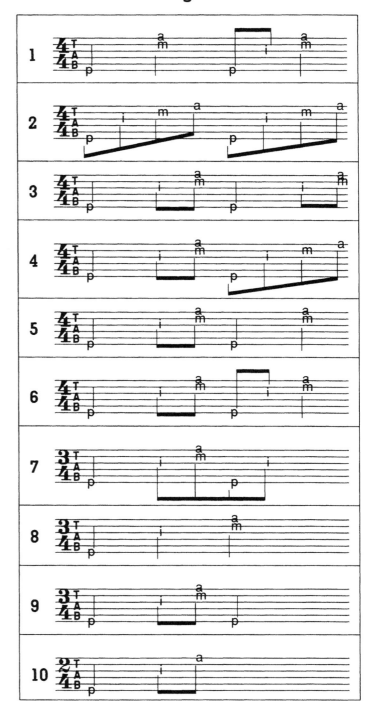

Chord Diagrams

	Major	Minor	Seventh
C			
C#/ Db			
D			
D#/ Eb			
E			
F			
F#/ Gb			
G			
G#/ Ab			
A			
A#/ Bb			
B			